To the journey
To time
To my mom
For the journals
And the passion

To my dad
For the art and knowledge
And sending poetry to my email
Once in a while

To Tom,
For the love
And the push to do what
I love

And to Mia,
For being my partner
In anything and everything.
And for dreaming
With me.

Thanks to Rupi Kaur,
For the inspiration, through yours I understood
My love for poetry.

And to me,

Thanks.

# WINTER SOLSTICE

LETTERS OF WONDERS, SELF LOVE AND BROKEN HEARTS.

HIGH TIDES AND LETTERS TO MY YOUNGER SELF.

LETTERS OF WONDERS, SELF LOVE AND BROKEN HEARTS.

Circumstantial coincidence

How easy is it to forget?

How lucky we are to see blue skies

Covered by green

Tree leaves

To write with a flower

All over their walls

To see their faces

Even when it

Seems like

The world has gone mad

I'm grateful

for the birds in the sky

That paint a picture as they fly by

For the songs that take me away

To Vienna, Tokyo, Argentina

Like a poem waiting for me to write

Those words

looking to hit

all those ears

It crosses by…

Waiting to inspire

The stories

waiting

to be made

And told


In crazy times

we must keep

bright sight

Take the bad

& bring out the good

from hard times

Those high tides


Is everything in life a coincidence?

Do we have a destiny

waiting to be met?

Is life just full of circumstance that turns into

Tragedy,

Opportunity?

How can we tell what's wrong or right?

How are we so fast to judge

or claim?

What 's the game?

Good

or bad…

Or keen

Or sad

Even with complete ignorance

To moral wrong

besides us

We've been taught

to turn our heads

To just pretend,

Evil crossing by our side

doesn't concern us.

Where does it all start?

Do we even remember

Where does it all go

What do we have?

& what do we know?

What have we lost?

What is even ours

and at what cost


where's all the time

that we spent

Or wasted?

Who's keeping a tab

Don't we have to let go

We have opportunities;

we have tons of loss

Everything happens for a reason

, and even If it doesn't

We are here to

make a reason

for it to happen.


It's all about circumstances;

The different endings

and outcomes

come  without

an end in mind.

We're here to find.

But what is the point of dwelling

on the past or

longing for a future

when all we are doing is


losing the moment?

What we said

We've had soulmates

We've felt pain

We've gone back

our hearts break

We thought we'd choke

We ran,

We felt

Our hearts like smoke

It had thorns

It's been sweet

We needed to meet

When time passes

We see rose glasses

We don't repent

We can't forget

The quicksand

The walks on the beach

The cheating

and lying

the toxic traits

the fish bait

thought it was great


All the lovers

All the "ones"

And those that got away

The loves of our lives

The ones with sharp knives


The stabs in the back

The broken hearts

The I want you backs

The husband to be

And the millions of plans

Left in day dreams

The one-night stands

All the blind sighs

Love flowed in tides

Sometimes mistaken

True love

Is it meant to be?

The drunken fights

All the highs

All the lows

All the starts

All the wars

All the laughs

The heartaches

And headaches

Bellyaches,


Broken hearts &

Healing thoughts

We can be friends

We'll never speak again

We'll break up

We'll make up


We can settle down

I felt like I could drown

So much sorrow

So much ache

All the stories

All the hate

Some with ends

Some descends

Some will leave, some will stay

We'll fly away

i know someday

we'll be okay

in

every

single

fucking

way.

Lost, potencial

Artist that paint

But don't see a finished painting

Writers that don't really get what

Their story is about

Singers that can't reach

The key quite right

Dancers that are afraid

of forgetting the next step

Don't worry,

take a chance

We're all

lost in this world

No one can figure out

who is right or wrong

What the answer is

What's enough and what's

too little

because even as all my words come together

it's hard to understand

what the point in all this is


if there is a suppose to

or a shouldn't

for realizing

There isn't really

an i couldn't


For better or for worse

No matter how much it hurts

Do whatever

The fuck

You want

We are here

To live

A cliche,

But live

You're best

Fucking

life.

For yourself.

No one else

You.

Find your

Most genuine you

In the loss and lost.

To let go

Of others thoughts.

Set you free.

And be

Whoever

The fuck

You

Want

To be.

Broken glass

Everyone reads the quotes

Oh, how wise

No one really understands

Until you're stuck in the moment

Can't believe

I can't breathe

It's unreal

When you see fragile glass

Shatter on the ground

Always trying to relate with everyone else

Making others dreams come true

But not seeing that the one that needs me the most

Is you...

The shape of worth

felt self-pity and insecurities

Rise from above

From within me

Relief

How can all this self-loathing

Unsettling hate

Towards the closest to me

Be so easy to let be

And to stay

And to hurt

But we always look for who to blame

To judge

That body

that face

But there is no one else to blame

You don't deserve to keep

this hate

And shame, in your heart

Why does it hurt so much?

When you see those, you love

Full of hate for themselves

They can't look at their reflection any longer

And it keeps getting harder

But how easy to look in the mirror

Everyday

Wasted energy on hating your reflection


How silly to believe your worth

Takes the shape of your body

Don't let yourself look back

Into the years

And have your stories

Not go on because you didn't jump in the deep oceans

From shame, fears of letting others see you

How you never got that bedazzled dressed

For new years

How you never let yourself

Feel sexy,

Or kinky

Or wild

You thought you better wait

Until your legs didn't jiggle

And your belly was flat

To crave a smaller size

To starve for 4 days straight

Or pray for sickness

To keep off that weight

Hate your appetite

Waiting for things you desire

Because you don't suit these society's standards

Absurd standards;

Release yourself from comparing

Stop promising a new diet every Monday

Or restrict your favorite foods on Friday

Swear next week you'll start a new training program

And cry after every fucking finished set.

Stop putting your body through things that don't bring joy

Just so you could take up a little less space in this world.

Loving others before loving yourself is so much easier,

it's easier to forgive loved ones

We are taught to love those around us

And to put others first

Giving a friendly hand to others doesn't mean you need to let others pull you down

Sometimes we need that hand more. To not want to look at our reflection and

change every fault caught through our eyes. To feel anger. Towards who knows

who. Feeling wrong for those flaws we think we own.

But whoever dared to tell us we are flawed. That we are broken.

What we are defined by. What makes us. whole.

Who gave anyone the right. To have a say.

and what looks right.

Our uniqueness

is our beauty

what's the hurry

what the goal.

We live in such a rush.

Can't keep up

we won't accept.

society will no longer dictate

how we love ourselves

and what's the shape

of our worth.

## Puzzling

We are not a puzzle

To be taken a part

No need

To find the missing part

We are put together.

We are not in pieces.

We are not broken.

We are not a game.

We are not a half

that needs to be completed,

We are whole.

Flashbacks

It's funny,

And strange

How our minds

Connect views

Smells tastes places

To emotions

We felt

We had

We shared

It's funny,

How our minds,

Our able to connect

Memories;

Seasons;

Periods;

We had

We lived

We shared

How seeing a forest

On my train ride

To the city

Our minds

Connect

To moments

On the other side of the world

All the way back to childhood years


Seasons of cold


Movements of fleeting happiness

Childhood recollections

How hearing a taste of a song

Will take us

All the way back to a long-lost love

A broken heart

Back to the sensation

incapability of being loved

Back to feelings of not being sufficient

Not being enough

Stopping us from hearing;

Listening

To melodies

Of hearts being shattered

Into millions of pieces

Tears that won't stop falling

And falling

Until the day that our heart went dry,

Empty

Tears are not to be found

Pain is a memory from the past.

How we broke

And put our pieces back together

Even better than before

And we actually realized

how we were always nothing but whole,

to see ourselves in parts.

Never pieces.

HIGH TIDES AND LETTERS TO MY YOUNGER SELF.

sail rides

ocean tides

It's seven to nine

you're safe & sound

lost & found

My heart pounds

No direction

lost orientation

lost at sea

for younger me,

those lost at sea

brought up

as victims

we fought

& we taught

our scars

and scares.

we shared

do you think

they even care?

on the bay

everyday my heart has broken

To see how sore

They left us…

you're insane

and insane i became

fish bait

how much has been taken away

without us even knowing

Without realizing it's even ours in the first place

How they've grown up stealing

While thinking it's theirs to take…

And when we feel empty or scared

And we think we need them for care,

To feel complete.

I could cry so many tears

until dry

for a younger me

That took so much hate

Craving for love

Thinking violence was it

safe & sound

all the abuse

my little heart could just not bear

for giving my love away

for not keeping my heart safe

for excusing him every time

Because i wanted to convince myself

That I needed to be loved by him,

by them

To be complete.

To give

And give

Being told if I don't give

Someone better, prettier

Will give instead

To feel replaceable

but to not want to be replaced

Its game

don't complain

don't lie

(or don't keep anything to yourself)


You're mine.

Those are the words I wanted to hear

But why be someone else's

When you,

yourself are home

You are enough.

You are love.

You are great.

You are yours.

your hearts at shore.

the deep blue sea

all i wanted was to be loved

to hear those,

I love you's

In his voice

little did I know

That the only I love you I needed

Was right inside me

deep in

the big blue sea

was all the love

I could ever need.

by the seashore

You made a mistake.

Forgive me.

I never wanted to hurt you.

Just take it.

You made a mistake.

Make it better,

take it all until you can't do it anymore.

Until you're on the shore

And you want to die.

You lose sight.

Can't stop to cry.

Pills won't take It away.

You can't run away.

Go home. You're not alone

Those old blades

Put them away.

notes in glass bottles

I hurt for my younger self.

Giving herself away.

Don't compare.

It 's not fair.

Your pain.

Our pain.

My pain.


I've made hope for us.

I won't lie.

there are hard nights

There are high tides.


Our heart is safe.

You're doing well.

You don't compare.

You try not to stare.

You're writing about self-love.

Not numbers on the scale

Our pain.

so deep

at sea.


wash off

those salty

worries

off your neck

Keep yourself

from the heavy ocean tide.

and finally

let yourself

at times,

have some

well fought

beach time.

Made in the USA
Columbia, SC
25 August 2021